Independence Hall

Ted and Lola Schaefer

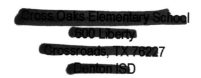
Heinemann Library
Chicago, Illinois

© 2006 Heinemann Library
a division of Reed Elsevier Inc.
Chicago, Illinois

Customer Service 888-454-2279

Visit our website at www.heinemannlibrary.com

Designed by Richard Parker and Mike Hogg Design
Illustrations by Jeff Edwards
Originated by Chroma Graphics (Overseas) Pte.Ltd
Printed and bound in China by South China Printing Company

12 11 10 09
10 9 8 7 6 5 4 3

Library of Congress Cataloging-in-Publication Data
Schaefer, Ted, 1948-
  Independence Hall / Ted and Lola M. Schaefer.
    p. cm. -- (Symbols of freedom)
  Includes index.
  ISBN 1-4034-6664-5 (library binding - hardcover) -- ISBN 1-4034-6673-4 (pbk.)
  ISBN 978-1-4034-6664-8 (library binding - hardcover) -- ISBN 978-1-4034-6673-0 (pbk.)
1. Independence Hall (Philadelphia, Pa.)--Juvenile literature. 2. United States--Politics and government--1775-1783-
-Juvenile literature. 3. United States--Politics and government--1783-1789--Juvenile literature. 4. Philadelphia (Pa.)--
Buildings, structures, etc.--Juvenile literature. I. Schaefer, Lola M., 1950- II. Title. III. Series.
  F158.8.I3S34 2005
  974.8'11--dc22
                            2005002035

Acknowledgments
The publishers would like to thank the following for permission to reproduce photographs:
Alamy pp. 12 (David Pattison); Bridgeman Art Library pp. 6, 11, 22 (© Atwater Kent Museum of Philadelphia),
Corbis pp. 27 (Ariel Skelley), 10, 15, 24 (Bettman), 25 (Charles E. Rotkin), 4 (Dennis Degnan), 24; Getty Images
pp. 8, 13 (Hulton Archive), 23 (Time & Life Pictures); Library of Congress pp. 5, 7, 17, 19, 28, 29; Peter Newark's
Americana Pictures pp. 9, 14, 16, 18, 20.

Cover photograph of Independence Hall reproduced with permission of Getty Images/Taxi.

In recognition of the National Park Service Rangers who are always present at the memorials, offering general information and
interpretative tours. We thank you!

The author would like to give a special thank you to Phil Sheridan of Independence National Historic Park for his thorough research
and explanations.

Every effort has been made to contact copyright holders of any material reproduced in this book. Any omissions will be rectified in
subsequent printings if notice is given to the publishers.

The publishers and authors have done their best to ensure the accuracy and currency of all the information in this book, however, they
can accept no responsibility for any loss, injury, or inconvenience sustained as a result of information or advice contained in the book.

Some words are shown in bold, **like this.** You can find out
what they mean by looking in the glossary.

Contents

Independence Hall

Independence Hall is a famous **landmark** in Philadelphia, Pennsylvania. It is a two-story, brick building with a clock and **steeple**.

Our nation's **founding fathers** met in
Independence Hall. They talked about
important ideas. They wrote **documents** that
formed the government of the United States.

A Place to Meet

William Penn and the **colonists** of Pennsylvania wanted to meet and talk about laws. They formed the **Pennsylvania Assembly.** They needed a place to meet in Philadelphia.

In 1732 work began on a new building. It was finished in 1753 and named the Pennsylvania State House. It was the best building in all the **colonies**.

The Liberty Bell

The **Pennsylvania Assembly** ordered a large bell for the new State House. In 1753, the bell was hung high in the **steeple** so it could be heard across the city.

The **colonists** were proud of their **freedoms**. They put words on the bell that meant: Let everyone know that this is a place where people are free. Years later it was called the Liberty Bell.

Unfair Taxes!

King George III of Britain ruled all thirteen American **colonies**. The British government was not always fair to the **colonists**. It collected **taxes** on many things the people needed.

10

The colonists were unhappy with the taxes.
They sent letters to King George III. They
asked him if he could help make the tax
laws fair.

First Continental Congress

The First **Continental Congress** met in 1774 in Carpenters' Hall, near the Pennsylvania State House. Men came from twelve **colonies**. They talked about **taxes** and King George III.

These men worked on a list of freedoms they wanted called the **Declaration of Rights**. They mailed it to King George III. They wanted to make changes in a peaceful way.

13

Time For War

King George III did not answer the **colonists**. He kept **taxing** them and sending more British soldiers to America. The colonists wanted **independence** from Britain.

Americans first fought British soldiers in Massachusetts in April 1775. This was the beginning of the **Revolutionary War** and their fight for freedom.

Second Continental Congress

The Second **Continental Congress** met in May of 1775 in the State House. They voted to form an American army. They asked George Washington to be its **commander**.

Congress decided that the American **colonies** needed to become a free nation. They asked Thomas Jefferson and four other men to write the **Declaration of Independence**.

The Declaration of Independence

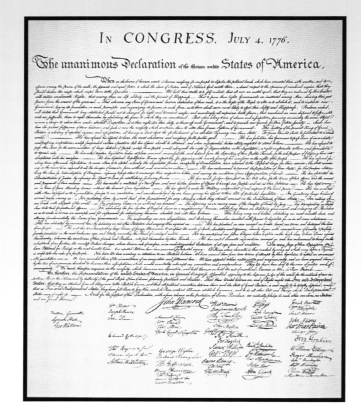

The **Declaration of Independence** said that King George III and Britain no longer ruled America. The thirteen **colonies** became the United States of America.

On July 4, 1776, the **Continental Congress** agreed on the Declaration of Independence. Four days later, they read it to a crowd gathered outside the State House. People cheered. The bell rang.

The U.S. Constitution

The Second **Continental Congress** also met in the State House. In 1787, the men wrote the United States **Constitution**.

20

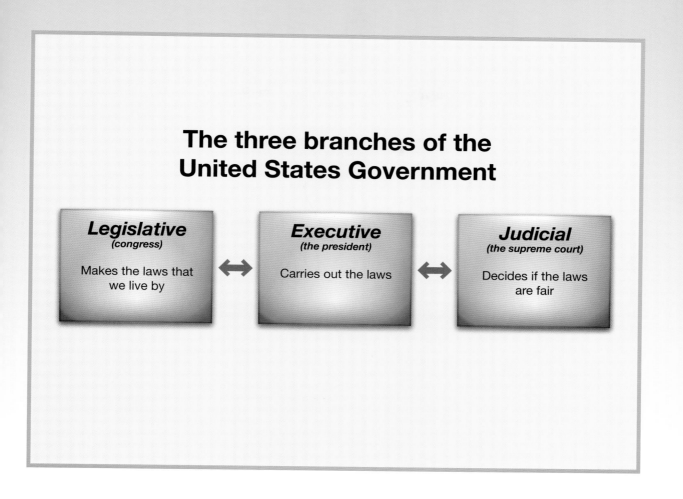

The three branches of the
United States Government

Legislative (congress)		Executive (the president)		Judicial (the supreme court)
Makes the laws that we live by	⟷	Carries out the laws	⟷	Decides if the laws are fair

The Constitution divided the U.S. government into three different parts. Each part had its own job. It also gave powers to the state and local governments.

21

The State House in Later Years

In 1799 the Pennsylvania state capital moved to the city of Lancaster. The Pennsylvania State House was not in use. Charles Peale rented part of the building.

Charles Peale was an artist. He painted
pictures of famous **statesmen** and hung them
on the walls. In 1802 the State House
became a museum.

Independence National Historic Park

Philadelphia bought the State House in 1816 and used it for offices and courtrooms. People remembered what had happened in this building. It became known as **Independence** Hall.

In 1896, work began to **restore** the State House. In 1948, Congress created Independence National Historic Park. Independence Hall is part of the park.

Visiting Independence Hall

Here is a map of **Independence** National Historic Park. When you visit Independence Hall, you can see the ink-well used by the people who signed the **Constitution**.

When you see Independence Hall, think of the men who met there. Their important ideas led to the **freedom** and government that we still have today.

Independence Hall

★ Independence Hall has two main floors, a basement, and a **steeple**.

★ At first the Liberty Bell was called the State House Bell or Province Bell. Sometime about 1839 it was first called the Liberty Bell.

★ The Liberty Bell was made in London, England, in 1752. It cracked during a test ringing. It was then rebuilt in Pennsylvania.

★ From 1790 to 1800 Philadelphia was the capital of the United States. The U.S. Congress met in the County Courthouse near the Pennsylvania State House. In 1800, the capital moved to Washington, D.C.

Timeline

Independence Hall

★ 1753   Bell hung in Pennsylvania State House **steeple**

★ 1774   First **Continental Congress** meets in the Pennsylvania State House

★ 1816   Philadelphia buys the Pennsylvania State House

★ 1948   Congress creates the **Independence** National Historic Park

★ 1976   The Liberty Bell is removed from the steeple of Independence Hall and placed in its own building on the grounds of the Independence National Historic Park. This begins the United States Bicentennial Celebration.

★ 2003   The Bell is moved to its new home at the Liberty Bell Center in the south-west of Independence National Historic Park

Glossary

colony area or country that is controlled by another country

colonist someone who lives in a colony

commander someone who controls a group of people in the armed forces

Constitution system of laws in a country that state the rights of the people and the powers of the government

Continental Congress men from each of the colonies that united to protect their rights and complain about the unfair taxes from King George III

Declaration of Independence written announcement that the thirteen American colonies were free from British rule

Declaration of Rights written list asking Britain to recognize the rights of Americans

document piece of paper with something important written on it

founding fathers men who talked about and wrote the first documents of the United States government, such as the Declaration of Independence and the Constitution

freedom having the right to say, behave, or move around as you please

independence not belonging to other people or another country

landmark building or place of importance

Pennsylvania Assembly first group of men to govern, or control, the Pennsylvania colony

restore to bring back to original condition

Revolutionary War war of 1775–1783 in which the United States fought for freedom from British rule

statesman leader who works to do good for the people

steeple tall tower with a spire on top, built on the roof of a building

tax money that people and businesses must pay to their government

More Books to Read

An older reader can help you with these books:

Britton, Tamara L. *Independence Hall*. Edina, Minn.: ABDO, 2003.

Marcovitz, Hal. *Independence Hall*. Philadelphia, Pa.: Mason Crest, 2003.

Visiting the Memorial

Independence Hall is open all year. The hours are 9:00 A.M. to 5:00 P.M. Monday to Sunday. You do not have to pay to visit Independence Hall.

To ask for a brochure that includes a map of Independence National Historic Park, write to this address:

Public Affairs Office
Independence National Historic Park
143 S. Third St.
Philadelphia, PA 19106.

Index